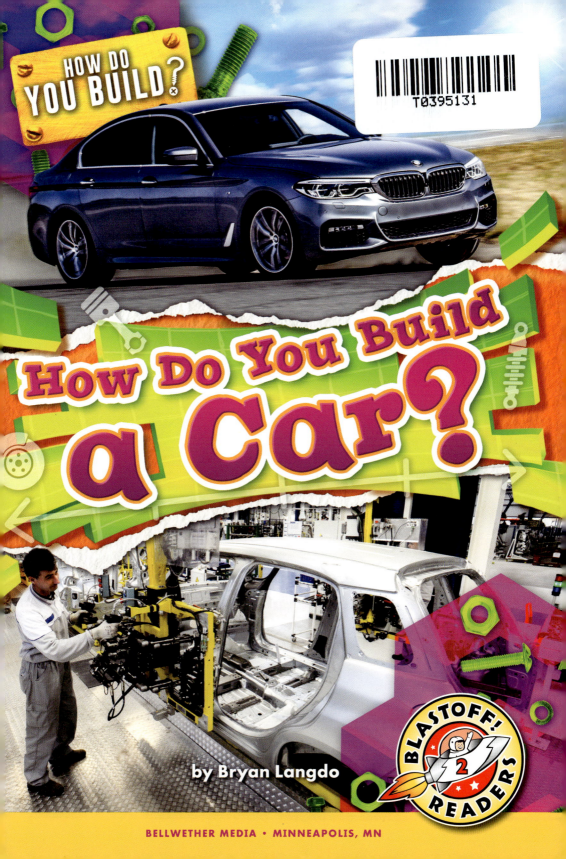

 **Blastoff! Readers** are carefully developed by literacy experts to build reading stamina and move students toward fluency by combining standards-based content with developmentally appropriate text.

 Level 1 provides the most support through repetition of high-frequency words, light text, predictable sentence patterns, and strong visual support.

 Level 2 offers early readers a bit more challenge through varied sentences, increased text load, and text-supportive special features.

 Level 3 advances early-fluent readers toward fluency through increased text load, less reliance on photos, advancing concepts, longer sentences, and more complex special features.

★ **Blastoff! Universe**

Reading Level

 Grade K  Grades 1–3  Grade 4

This edition first published in 2026 by Bellwether Media, Inc.

No part of this publication may be reproduced in whole or in part without written permission of the publisher. For information regarding permission, write to Bellwether Media, Inc., Attention: Permissions Department, 3500 American Blvd W, Suite 150, Bloomington, MN 55431.

Library of Congress Cataloging-in-Publication Data

LC record for How Do You Build a Car? available at: https://lccn.loc.gov/2025010698

Text copyright © 2026 by Bellwether Media, Inc. BLASTOFF! READERS and associated logos are trademarks and/or registered trademarks of Bellwether Media, Inc. Bellwether Media is a division of FlutterBee Education Group.

Editor: Rachael Barnes   Book Designer: Josh Brink

Printed in the United States of America, North Mankato, MN.

Table of Contents

On the Go — 4
Planning a Car — 6
On the Assembly Line — 10
A Finished Car — 20
Glossary — 22
To Learn More — 23
Index — 24

On the Go

A driver gets into their new car. They start the engine.

They hit the road in style!

Planning a Car

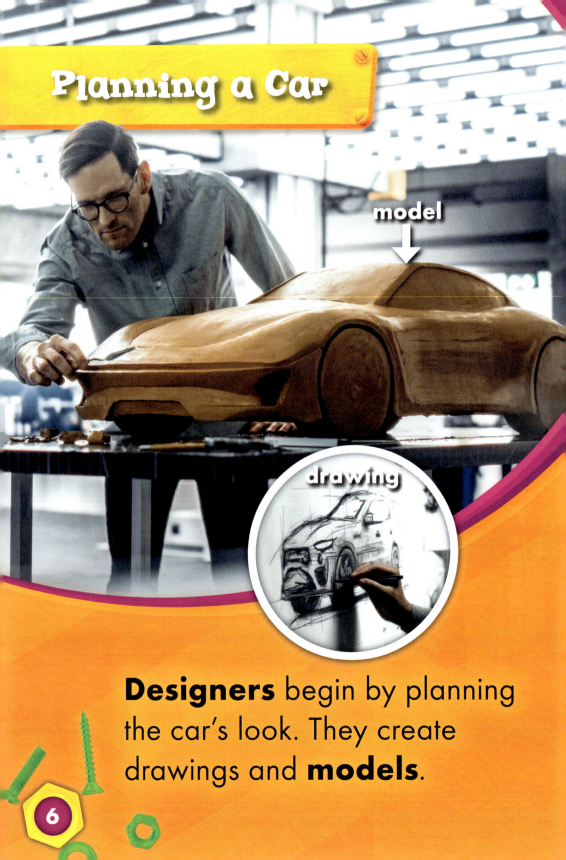

model

drawing

Designers begin by planning the car's look. They create drawings and **models**.

Engineers plan how the car will work. It takes years to design a car!

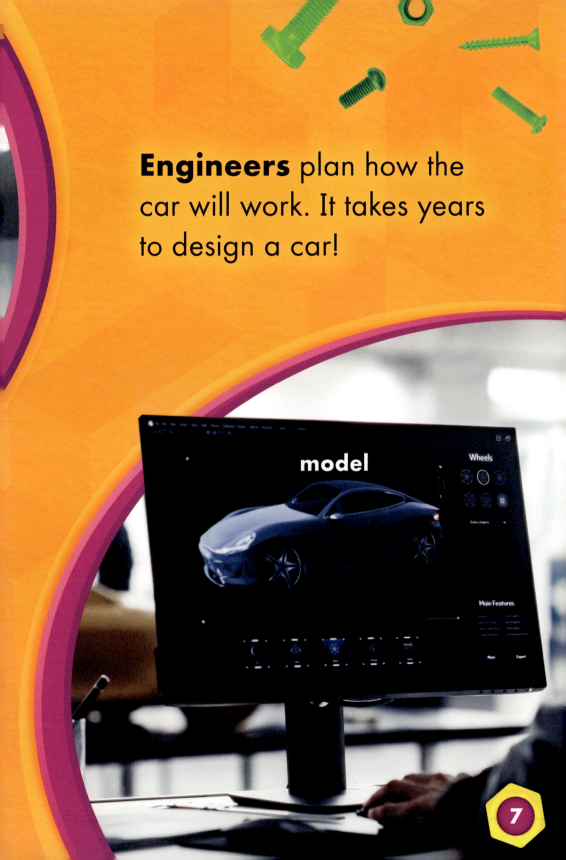

Cars are built on **assembly lines**. Car parts move along the line to different stations.

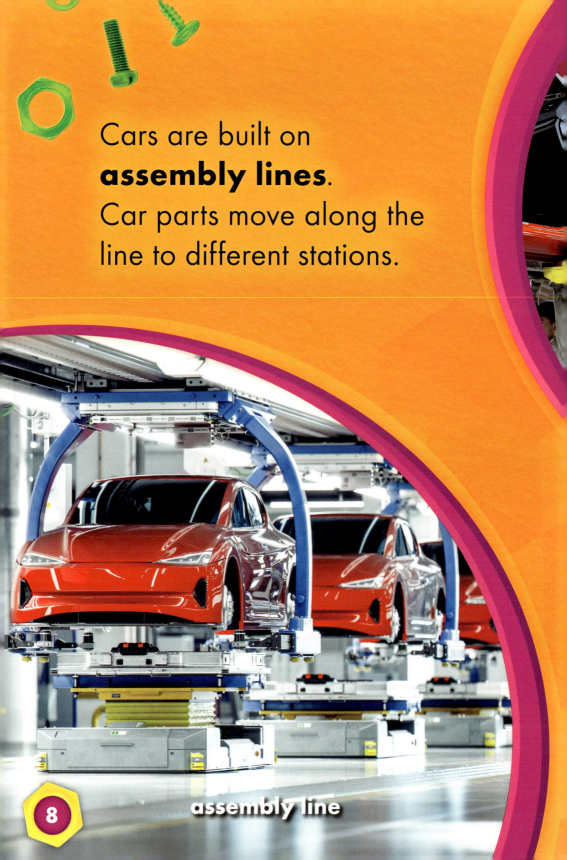

assembly line

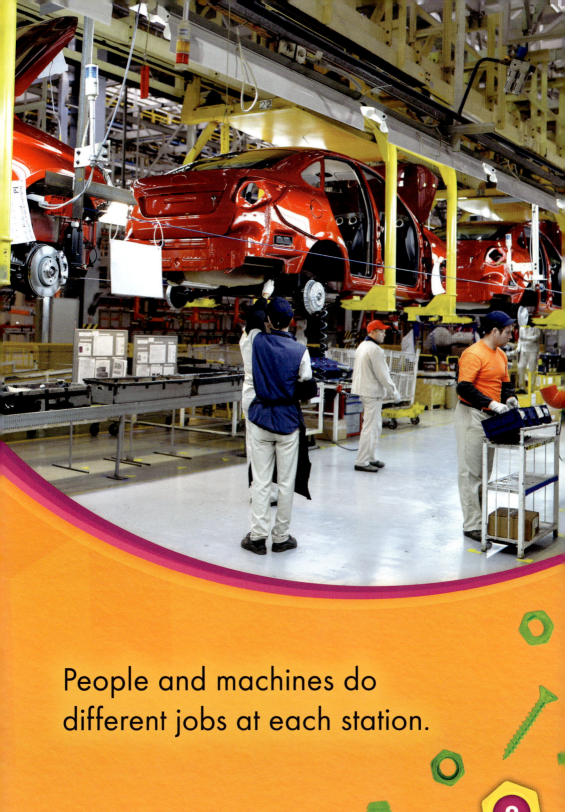

People and machines do different jobs at each station.

On the Assembly Line

die

First, machines move steel sheets into a huge **press**. The press pushes the metal into **dies**.

This shapes the steel into parts of a car body.

What Do You Need?

steel

paint

plastic

glass

rubber

11

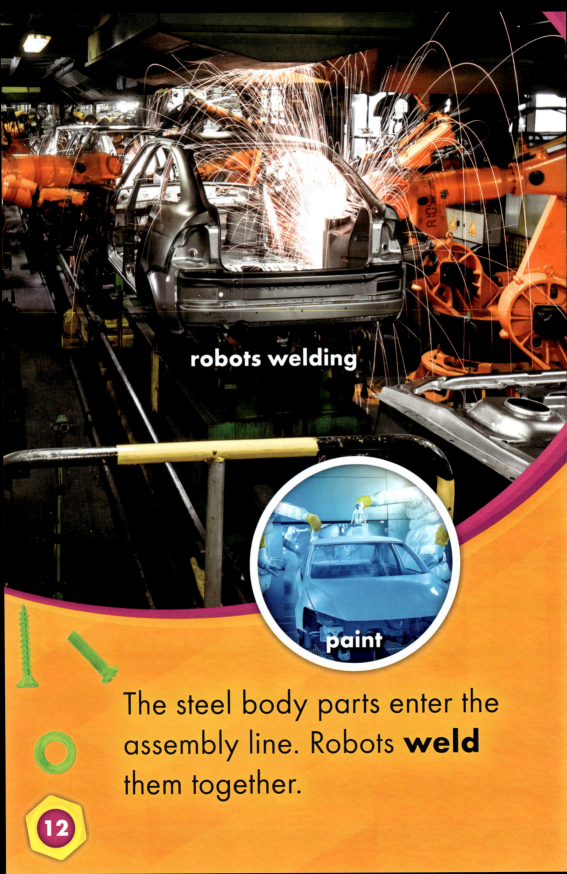

robots welding

paint

The steel body parts enter the assembly line. Robots **weld** them together.

12

Then robots paint the car bodies.

Parts of a Car

- doors
- windows
- engine
- wheels
- body

Workers put in the engine and brakes. They also add other parts under the car.

Inside the car, workers add **electrical wiring**.

electrical wiring

axle

Workers put in the steering wheel and plastic dashboard. They connect wheels and rubber tires to **axles**.

The car gets **bumpers** and glass windows. Workers put in seats, too!

Bugatti Chiron Super Sport 300+

Cost more than $3.8 million

Top speed 304.773 miles (490.5 kilometers) per hour

Built in Molsheim, France

Famous for one of the fastest cars in the world

The car is almost done. Workers run tests on it.

✓ Step by Step ✓

1. Designers and engineers make plans.

2. A press pushes steel sheets into dies.

3. Workers and robots weld and paint car body parts.

4. Workers put in the engine and other parts under the car.

5. Electrical wiring goes inside the car.

6. Workers inspect the car.

They **inspect** the brakes and other parts. They make sure the car is safe to drive.

A Finished Car

Companies send cars to be sold. Some cars are fast.

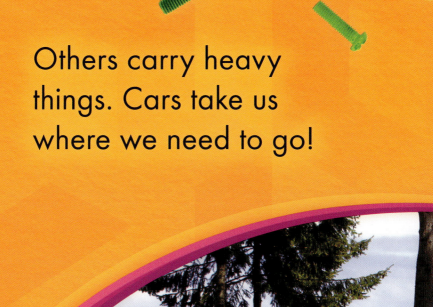

Others carry heavy things. Cars take us where we need to go!

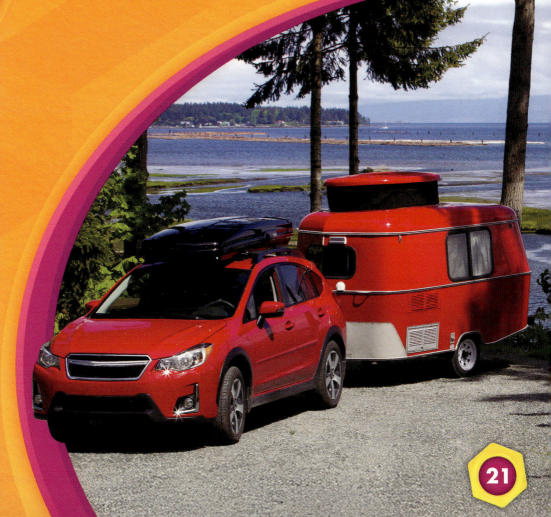

Glossary

assembly lines—arrangements of workers or machines where parts pass from one station to the next until a product is put together

axles—bars that wheels turn on

bumpers—plastic bars at the front and back of a car

designers—people who make a plan for a car or other type of vehicle

dies—tools that are used to shape metal

electrical wiring—a system of wires that carry power used to run machines

engineers—people who are trained to design and build machines, systems, or structures

inspect—to check something to make sure it works correctly

models—small versions of cars or other structures; models can be physical or digital.

press—a machine that shapes something by pushing down on it

weld—to join pieces together by melting metal

To Learn More

AT THE LIBRARY

Gunzi, Christiane. *Cars*. New York, N.Y.: Gareth Stevens Publishing, 2024.

Klepeis, Alicia Z. *Superfast Cars*. Minneapolis, Minn.: Jump!, 2022.

Murray, Laura K. *Mechanics*. Mankato, Minn.: Creative Education and Creative Paperbacks, 2023.

ON THE WEB

Factsurfer.com gives you a safe, fun way to find more information.

1. Go to www.factsurfer.com.
2. Enter "car" into the search box and click 🔍.
3. Select your book cover to see a list of related content.

Index

assembly lines, 8, 12
axles, 16
body, 11, 12, 13
brakes, 14, 19
Bugatti Chiron Super
    Sport 300+, 17
bumpers, 17
companies, 20
dashboard, 16
designers, 6
dies, 10
drawings, 6
driver, 4
electrical wiring, 14
engine, 4, 14
engineers, 7
inspect, 19
models, 6, 7
paint, 12, 13
parts, 8, 11, 12, 14, 19
parts of a car, 13
press, 10
road, 4

robots, 12, 13
seats, 17
stations, 8, 9
steel, 10, 11, 12
steering wheel, 16
step by step, 19
tests, 18
tires, 16
weld, 12
what do you need?, 11
wheels, 16
windows, 17
workers, 14, 16, 17, 18

The images in this book are reproduced through the courtesy of: Yauhen_D, cover (top hero); Nikola Fific, cover (bottom hero); JDzacovsky, pp. 2-3; WildSnap, pp. 4-5; Gorodenkoff, pp. 6, 7; Frame Stock Footage, p. 6 (drawing); IM Imagery, p. 8; Sergej Cash, pp. 8-9; Bert Hoferichter/ Alamy, p. 10; Nuttawut Uttamaharad, p. 11 (steel); funfunphoto, p. 11 (paint); piyaset, p. 11 (plastic); Studio Peace, p. 11 (glass); nordroden, p. 11 (rubber); Andrei Kholmov, pp. 12, 19 (step four), 20-21; Jenson, p. 12 (paint); Andrius Kaziliunas, p. 13 (engine); PuccaPhotography, p. 13 (mustang); yacobchuk, p. 14; OVKNHR, pp. 14-15; Adam Berry/ Getty Images, p. 16; Bastian/ Alamy, p. 16 (axles); Martyn Lucy/ Getty Images, p. 17; dpa picture alliance/ Alamy, pp. 18-19; gerenme, p. 19 (step two); supergenijalac, p. 19 (step three); Aleksandr Potashev, p. 19 (step five); Jenson, p. 19 (step six); oksana.perkins, p. 21; Roman Vasilenia, pp. 22-23, 24 (background car); Brandon Woyshnis, p. 23.

24